The Chosen One

Contents

The Chosen One

Peter Leigh

Published in association with
The Basic Skills Agency

Hodder & Stoughton

A MEMBER OF THE HODDER HEADLINE GROUP

Acknowledgements
Cover: Fred Van Deelan
Illustrations: Brian Lee

Orders: please contact Bookpoint Ltd, 78 Milton Park, Abingdon, Oxon OX14
4TD. Telephone: (44) 01235 827720, Fax: (44) 01235 400454. Lines are open
from 9.00–6.00, Monday to Saturday, with a 24-hour message answering service.
Email address: orders@bookpoint.co.uk

British Library Cataloguing in Publication Data
A catalogue record for this title is available from The British Library

ISBN 0 340 80236 7

First published 2001
Impression number   10 9 8 7 6 5 4 3 2 1
Year   2007 2006 2005 2004 2003 2002 2001

Copyright © 2001 Peter Leigh

Typeset by SX Composing DTP, Rayleigh, Essex.
Printed in Great Britain for Hodder & Stoughton Educational, a division of
Hodder Headline Plc, 338 Euston Road, London NW1 3BH, by Athenaeum
Press, Gateshead, Tyne & Wear.

1

The Phone

Adam was carrying a box.
He was carrying it as if it was a winning
Lottery ticket.
He put it down carefully on the table.
'Great!' he said.
'I've got one! I've finally got one!
What I've always wanted!'

He began to unwrap the box.
'I'm so excited. I can hardly wait.
It's so cool,' he said.

It was a mobile phone – the best you can buy!
'Oh yes!' he said. 'It's perfect! Perfect!
Look at that plastic,' he said.
'That's quality plastic, that is!
Only top people have phones like this.'

He put it to his ear.
He started to think about all the things
he could do with the phone.
'Smith! You're fired! Pack your bags and go! …
Yes, Britney? Tonight, Britney? Of course.

'Oh brilliant, brilliant, brilliant!
I should have bought one years ago.
Now, what do I do next?
Oh yes, charge the phone.'

Suddenly the phone rang.
Adam looked at it, surprised.
'I haven't even charged the phone yet.'

The phone still rang.
It was glowing with a strange, green light.
Adam picked it up, and held it to his ear.

'Hello? Is there anyone there? Hello?'
There was silence.
'It must be a fault. Oh well …'

Suddenly a voice spoke. 'Adam?'

'Yes?' said Adam.

'Is that Adam, son of Man?'
said the strange voice.

'Well, son of Ken, as a matter of fact.
But he is a man.
Look, who are you? What do you want?'

'Adam, son of Man …
you are the chosen one!'

'What do you mean – the chosen one?
Chosen for what?
Look here! Who is this?'

But the line had gone dead.

'Hello? Is anyone there?
Is this some kind of joke?
It's completely dead.
It must have been some sort of fault.
Never mind! Where was I?
Oh yes! The phone charger.'

He pulled the charger from the box
and carefully fitted it into the phone.

'Good. Now, what's next?'

He picked up the instruction sheet.

'Attach the charger to the phone.
Put the charger in the plug socket.
Well, I've done that. What's next?
Switch on, and make your first call.
I know! I'll call Mum.
She's always saying I should ring her more.'

Adam tapped out a number on the phone.
'Nothing! No ringing, no nothing!
This damn phone …
Perhaps the charger is not working.

But it's turned on at the wall
and the phone is charged.
It must be the phone.'

He threw it angrily back into the box.
Suddenly the phone rang again.
It glowed with the same green light.

'Hello?' said Adam.

It was the voice.
'Adam, son of Man. We are coming.
Soon, very soon, we shall be with you.'

'Look! What is this?' said Adam angrily.

'We come from beyond the stars.
Swifter than starlight we come.
And we are coming for you!'

'For me? Why me?'

'Because, Adam, son of Man,
you are the chosen one!'
'Chosen? Chosen for what?'

'To tell your world that we are coming.
To tell your world that it is finished.
To tell your world that it is ours.'

'What? But … but, who are you?'

'Who are we?'

'Yes! You ring me up,
and tell me all these things.
But I don't know you. Who are you?'

'We are the Masters of the Universe!'

'What do you mean? Masters of the Universe?
Look! Who is this?'

But the line had gone dead.

'Right!' said Adam. 'That does it.
I'm taking this straight back to the shop!
Masters of the Universe, indeed!'

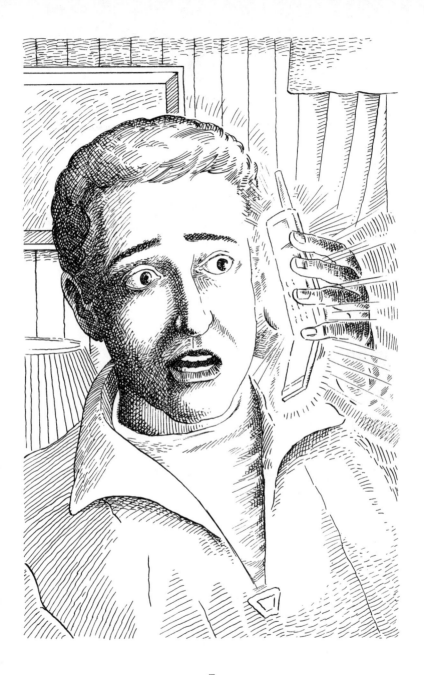

2

The Shop

Adam crashed the phone down
in front of the salesman.
'I bought this phone from you this morning,'
shouted Adam.
'And it doesn't work!'

'Perhaps sir forgot to charge the phone?'

'Sir did not forget to charge the phone.
It's the phone. It's no good.'

'Yes sir, but it was fine this morning.
Perhaps you've done something not quite right.
Mobile phones can be tricky at first.'

'Look, I don't find them tricky.
And I haven't done something not quite right.
It's the phone, I tell you!'

'Perhaps if you would like to give it me,
I could take a look at it.'

Adam gave him the phone.

'Thank you. Now let me see.
Battery charged? Yes, it's fine.
It seems to be in perfect working order.
Perhaps you would like to make a call?'

He handed the phone back to Adam.

'But it won't work!
See, what did I tell you?
It's … Oh … it's ringing.
Well, it may be ringing now, but …
Oh, hello … Yes, hello Mum … Yes, it's me.
… Yes, this is my new phone …
… Yes, I know they're expensive, Mum …
… Yes, I know you're only
two minutes away, but …
Look, sorry Mum. I've got to go now!'

Adam ended the call.
The salesman was smiling at him.

'There we are, sir.
What did I say? It's perfectly OK.'

'But it was dead earlier on.'

'Of course it was, sir.
People often have problems at first,
until they get used to them.'

'But it wasn't that … and …
what about that joke?'

'Joke, sir?'

'Yes, you know. The voice from outer space.'

'You had a call from outer space?'

'Yes. Saying it's the end of the world.
From the Masters of the Universe.
They knew my name and everything.'

'Well, they would do, wouldn't they, sir, them being Masters of the Universe?'
'Look, it's not funny.'

'No, sir! It's not funny at all.
But you say this was before it was even switched on?'

'Yes.'

'So there couldn't have been any power?'

'No.'

There was a long pause.

Finally he said, 'Well, I don't think you'll have any problems now.
Everything's working fine.'

He opened the door for Adam.

'If you do have any more
of those phone calls,' he said,
'I suggest you ring the police.
Goodbye, sir!'

And he closed the door behind Adam.

'Nutter!' he said under his breath,
as Adam walked away.

3

The Police

'He didn't believe me,' he said.
'I'll ring Mum again.
Just to check it's still working.'

He tapped out a number on the phone.

'Nothing! It's dead again.
That salesman … I'll kill him'

The phone suddenly rang.
He answered it.

'Hello, Mum? Is that you …?'

'Adam, son of Man ...'

'Oh, not you again.
Leave me alone, or I'll get the police
on to you.'

'The police?' said the voice.

'Yes, the police.
There's a law against unwanted phone calls.'

'I see. The police make your laws, do they?'

'Well, not exactly.
But they make sure everybody obeys them.'

'And you think they will make us obey them?'

'Yes.'

You know even less than we thought, Adam.
All your police, and all your armies,
could never stand against us.'

'I'm not listening to any more of this.
I'm putting the phone down right now.'

'DO NOT! Listen, Adam, son of Man.
You are a little, little people.
But we are great,
far, far greater than you can imagine.
You are foolish, weak and stupid ...'

'WHAT?'

'We have studied you.
You put poisons into the air and into the water.'

'Well, yes there is a bit of pollution.'

'You burn your green places.
You kill other creatures for food.'

'All right! Yes, there are some problems,
but it's not that bad ...'

'We cannot understand these things, Adam.
Why do you do them?
How can you be so backward?'

'Well, I don't know ... It's just that ... Well ...'

'It does not matter.
It is not your world now, Adam.
It is our world.'

'What ... What do you mean?'

'Adam, do you still not understand?
We are coming to your world.
We, the Masters of the Universe,
and Lords of all things, are coming.
Your time has ended.'

'No, it can't be ...'

'You cannot stand in our way.
You are such a little, little people.
To you we are gods!
And we are close now, very close.
We can see your world now.
It is filling our screens.'

'You have only one chance.
The task for which you have been chosen.
Have you done it yet?
Have you told them of our coming?'

'Well, no, I haven't …'

'Then you must! It is nearly too late!
Adam, son of Man, if you fail in this,
you are finished!
You and all your people!'

'What? But what can I do? Hello? … Hello? …'
But the phone had gone dead.

'It must be a joke,' he said to himself.
'It's a telephone threat, that's what it is.
The salesman said to phone the police.'

Quickly he tapped out a number.
'Hello, is that the police station?'

'Yes sir,' said a voice the other end.
'What can I do for you?'

'I keep getting threatening phone calls.'

'And what is the nature of these threats?
What are you being threatened with?'

'The end of the world.
I keep getting phone calls
from this voice,
and it says that I am the chosen one,
and that they are coming,
and I've got to tell the world about it.
And they're the Masters of the Universe.'

'It sounds like someone is playing a joke, sir.
You should be careful
who you give your number to.'

'But that's just it. I've only just got the phone.
I haven't given the number to anybody.
And the calls come when the phone's off.'

'When the phone's off?'

'Yes, or when the battery is not charged.'

'That's some phone you have there, sir!
I wouldn't complain about it if I were you.
Find out how it works
and you could make yourself a million.'

'Look, this isn't funny.
The phone works when I don't want it to,
and doesn't when I do.'

'Well, it's working now, isn't it?
Look, sir, this is a police station,
not a phone repair shop.
Nor have we got time to sort out silly jokes!
Now, I suggest you take your phone
back to the shop, or throw it in the river.
I don't care!
But stop wasting our time
with silly phone calls!'

'But, officer …'

'Before I get angry!'

4

The Space
Telescope

The call ended.
But before Adam could do anything,
the phone rang again.

Adam answered nervously. 'Yes?'

It was the voice.
'We are close now, Adam, son of Man.
Our ship is vast.
Already it must be filling your skies.'

Adam rushed to the window.
The sky was blue and empty.
A little kitten was playing on the grass.
'I can't see anything,' said Adam.
'There's only a kitten playing on the grass.'

'This is your last chance,' said the voice.
'To tell the world of our coming.
Do it now!'
And the line went dead.

'But ... I can't see anything,' said Adam.
'It must be a joke ... but ... supposing it's not?
How do I tell?
I know! There's that big telescope outside town.
They must know if there's a huge spaceship
heading towards us.'

He tapped out a number on the phone.

A voice answered. 'Hello?'

'Hello, is that the space telescope?'

'Well, not the telescope itself. Just the operator.'

'Listen, I don't have time for jokes.
There's a huge spaceship heading towards us.'

'Oh no, not another one.'

'Another one?'

'Yes, we've had five this week.
What's yours?
Time lords, is it? Or Martians?
Or is it Masters of the Universe?'

'Well, it's Masters of the Universe.'

'See, what did I tell you?'

'But they say they're in a huge spaceship
heading straight for us.
You must be able to see it in your telescope.'

'There's nothing in my telescope.'

'But are you sure? Perhaps you missed it.'

'I haven't missed anything.
Listen, I can see a stone fall on the Moon.
I can see a puff of dust on Mars.
I can see anything bigger than
a table-tennis ball.
And there is nothing there.'

'But are you quite sure?'

'Listen, let me repeat it.
If it's space,
and if it's bigger than a table-tennis ball,
this telescope will see it.
And there is nothing out there!
You've been watching too many *X-Files*.'

And he hung up.

5

The End?

'Perhaps he's right,' said Adam to himself.
'Perhaps there is nothing.
But who were those calls from, then?
And why …?'

The phone rang again.
Adam hesitated, then picked it up.

'Hello?'

'Adam, son of Man, it is too late.
We have landed.

Look out now, Adam,
and you will see a sight to amaze you.'

Adam rushed to the window, and looked out.

'But there's nothing there, I tell you.
There's just the kitten playing on the grass.'

'We are landed.
Your world is over now, Adam.
We are here with all our vast power.
We are … What?
Something is wrong.
What is happening?
Something is rocking the ship.
What is happening? Adam?'

'Nothing's happening, I tell you.
Just the kitten playing with something
that it has found.
Looks like a table-tennis ball.'

'... The ship ... It is being destroyed ...
but what could do this?
Oh! I cannot believe it ...
It is a monster, such a monster.
I have never seen such a monster ... It's huge.
Why did you not tell us, Adam,
that there are such monsters in your world?'

'But there's nothing there.
Just the kitten playing.'

'It is ripping the ship apart ...
Such teeth, such claws.
We will all die ... Aaaah!'

The phone suddenly went dead.

'What do you mean?' shouted Adam.
'There are no monsters.
Just the kitten, and it's stopped now.
Where are you?'

But there was only silence!

Suddenly the phone rang again.
Adam stared at it, and then answered it.

'Hello?'

'Oh hello, Adam,' said the salesman.
'This is the phone shop here.
Just checking that your phone is OK now.
Well, it seems to be in perfect order now.
Adam? …
Are you there? … Adam?'